PERSONAL FINANCE FOR BEGINNERS GUIDE TO MUTUAL FUNDS

Copyright 2017

Table of Contents

Introduction

Mutual Funds

Invest

Types of Mutual Funds

Mutual Fund Prospectus

Mutual Fund Research

401(k) and 403(b) Plans

The Powers of Compounding Money

The Powers of Compounding Money II

Summary

Additional Resources

DISCLAIMER: this book is not intended to be construed as investment advice.

To my family and friends

'Rule No.1: Never lose money. Rule No.2: Never forget rule No.1'

~ **Warren Buffett**

Introduction

This book is a helpful guide to understanding mutual funds. Inside this book is information to help out the average investor, as well as the expert.

This book will discuss some of the types of mutual funds, what a prospectus is, mutual fund research tools and also workplace-sponsored retirement plans. The last section discusses the powers of

compounding money

Mutual Funds

It is good idea to begin to save money as early as one can due to the powers of compounding money. Compounding money creates passive income, that is, one doesn't have to work actively while creating a separate stream or source of income.

With those savings, enroll into an automatic savings plan and have the money deposited into your checking or savings account at your bank or credit union. Do this once a month. In five, ten, twenty years from now you will thank yourself for doing so.

Invest

Next invest your savings by dollar cost averaging into mutual funds that have a good track record and low expense ratios. Dollar-cost-averaging is simply investing a fixed amount of money weekly, bi-weekly, monthly, etc.

Mutual funds pool and manage money from investors and invest the money into the stock and / or bond markets. There are three types of mutual funds, growth funds, income funds and hybrid funds. Each fund serves a different purpose and objective for different investors

Types of Mutual Funds

As mentioned in the previous section, mutual funds can be divided into three types; growth funds, income funds and hybrid funds. Each one of these funds can suit different needs or objectives for different individuals.

A growth fund will generally invest in just stocks. With a growth fund, it is best to invest your money in the fund for a long period of time, such as over five years or more. Over the long run, growth funds will outperform income and hybrid funds, but they are more risky and volatile in the short term. Typically people who are not approaching retirement and can take on more risk will find these funds more suitable than an income fund.

An income fund typically invests in bonds or high paying dividends paid from stocks. Income funds are less risky than growth and hybrid funds. Income funds regularly pay interest and / or dividends to the investor once a month or every quarter (for example, every three months); hence income funds are generally more stable than growth and hybrid funds, but have less potential for price appreciation. Retirees are more likely to find these types of funds more suitable to meet their objectives.

Some mutual funds are classified as hybrid funds; that is, they have the characteristics of both growth funds and income funds. Those funds are typically less volatile than growth funds and more volatile than income funds. They are suited to the investor who wants some stock market appreciation as well as interest and dividend payouts

Mutual Fund Prospectus

The different types of mutual funds offered by a mutual fund company will be listed in a document called a prospectus. The prospectus typically contains financial and risk information of each mutual fund available by the company managing the mutual funds.

The prospectus shows the historic performance and expense ratios of each mutual fund. The lower the expense ratio, the better the mutual fund company is doing at managing the costs of running the operation of the mutual fund. Diversify your money among the best funds available or the ones that suit your objectives and needs.

Mutual Fund Research

If you want to do mutual research analysis on your own, then try visiting Morningstar, Inc's website Morningstar.com. Morningstar is a financial company that specializes in investment research and provides research tools to help a person to analyze some of the thousands of mutual funds available.

Morningstar provides historic financial information, charts, fund performance and information about the management team of the mutual funds. Financial information such as asset allocation (the percentage of money that the mutual fund is invested in stocks and bonds), dividend yields, dividend payouts, and more, is provided.

Morningstar also provides a percentage breakout of which sectors and industries that the mutual funds are invested in. Charts detail and show which industry the mutual funds are invest in by every industry imaginable (banks, internet, oil, restaurants, grocery stores, retail / clothing stores, to name a few).

401(k) and 403(b) Plans

If your employer offers a workplace sponsored retirement plan such as a 401(k) or 403(b)), enroll in it as soon as you can. Essentially that is a bonus that you should take advantage of; because your employer will match your contribution dollar for dollar up to a certain percentage of gross income. Enroll in the plan and invest automatically during each bi-weekly pay period.

As mentioned, many workplace retirement plans match dollar-for-dollar what you save, up to 6% of gross income in many cases. For example, if your gross income is $2,000.00 a pay period, you can invest up to 6% (or $120.00) a pay period and your company will match the amount, $120.00.

Your employer will typically offer a list of mutual funds available for selection in the prospectus that is provided by the company managing the mutual funds. Look at each mutual fund in the prospectus to determine the best rates of returns and expense ratios. Diversify your money among the best funds available or the ones that suit your needs.

The Powers of Compounding Money

Also understand the powers of compounding money. Depending upon the rate of return and time (e.g., years) that you have to invest, your money can grow significantly. For example, if you start today with $10,000.00, and the money that you invest compounds at a rate of 5% a year, in twenty years you will have around **$25,000.00**. But since 5% is a conservative return, image the following scenarios:

- If you start today with $10,000.00, and the money that you invest compounds at a rate of 10% a year, in twenty years you will have around **$61,000.00**.

- If you start today with $10,000.00, and the money that you invest compounds at a rate of 15% a year, in twenty years you will have around **$142,000.00**.

- If you start today with $10,000.00, and the money that you invest compounds at a rate of 20% a year, in twenty years you will have around **$319,000.00!**

- Or if you start today with $10,000.00, and the money that you invest compounds at a rate of 25% a year, in twenty years you will have around **$693,000.00!**

- Or take an extreme example: if you start today with $10,000.00, and the money that you invest compounds at a rate of 50% a year, in forty years you will have around **$73,715,548,806.27!**

* These scenarios assume no added money and capital, and assumes no taxes.

The Powers of Compounding Money II

How about if you add $500.00 a month, or $1,000.00 a month in addition to the $10,000.00 that you started out with? If you start today with $10,000.00, add $500.00 a month to invest, and the money that you invest compounds at an annual rate of 10% a year, in twenty years you will have around **$89,000.00**.

If you start today with $10,000.00, add $500.00 a month to invest, add $500.00 a month to invest, and the money that you invest compounds at an annual rate of 15% a year, in twenty years you will have around **$193,000.00**.

If you start today with $10,000.00, add $500.00 a month to invest, and the money that you invest compounds at an annual rate of 20% a year, in twenty years you will have around **$412,000.00!**

Or if you start today with $10,000.00, add $500.00 a month to invest, and the money that you invest compounds at an annual rate of 25% a year, in twenty years you will have around **$864,000.00!**

Or take an extreme example: if you start today with $10,000.00, add $500.00 a month to invest, and the money that you invest compounds at an annual rate of 50% a year, in forty years you will have around

$84,772,879,627.21!

Based on the scenarios above, some of the hypothetical outcomes are below if you add $1,000.00 a month:

If you start today with $10,000.00, add $1,000.00 a month to invest, and the money that you invest compounds at an annual rate of 10% a year, in twenty years you will have around **$117,000.00**.

If you start today with $10,000.00, add $1,000.00 a month to invest and the money that you invest compounds at an annual rate of 15% a year, in twenty years you will have around **$243,000.00**.

If you start today with $10,000.00, add $1,000.00 a month to invest and the money that you invest compounds at an annual rate of 20% a year, in twenty years you will have around **$505,000.00!**

Or if you start today with $10,000.00, add $1,000.00 a month to invest and the money that you invest compounds at an annual rate of 25% a year, in twenty years you will have around **$1,035,000.00!**

Or take an extreme example: if you start today with $10,000.00, add $1,000.00 a month to invest and the money that you invest compounds at an annual rate of 50% a year, in forty years you will have around $73,715,548,806.27!

Again, these scenarios assume no added money and capital, and assumes no taxes.

There are also two books available on compounding money (The Powers of Compounding Money and also The Powers of Compounding Money II) at the links that follow. Detailed charts are available that show how much one can make over a long period of time with a small amount of money at varying rates of returns. The first book is for beginners and the second book discusses more advanced topics, the links for the books follow:

The Powers of Compounding Money

http://amzn.to/2wGXTJ9

The Powers of Compounding Money II

http://amzn.to/2wJmBH5

Summary

After you have paid yourself first, invest your savings in a mutual fund or mutual funds suited to your needs and objectives. Employ dollar-cost-averaging bi-weekly or weekly.

Be sure you understand how to choose and research a mutual fund depending upon your needs and objectives by reading the prospectus and Morningstar.com.

To find a mutual fund with a good track record, you can find the rates of returns by reading the mutual fund's prospectus. Compare those returns to the other mutual funds and diversify your money among the best performing mutual funds offered or diversify your money among the mutual funds that best suit your needs and objectives.

Also take advantage of your company's 401 (k) and 403 (b) workplace sponsored retirement plans if one is offered.

Both plans offer tax breaks and matching by your employer

And lastly, understand the importance of the powers of compounding money.

DISCLAIMER: this book is not intended to be construed as investment advice.

ADDITIONAL RESOURCES

LINKS TO BOOKS

The Powers of Compounding Money

http://amzn.to/2wGXTJ9

The Powers of Compounding Money II

http://amzn.to/2wJmBH5

AUTHOR'S YOUTUBE CHANNELS

https://www.youtube.com/channel/UCq7uNSjONd6E8tsvErAHqNQ

https://www.youtube.com/channel/UC9xoY04t1q4whrjPjf2b0Uw

AUTHOR'S BLOGS

https://thestockmarketinvestorblog.blogspot.com

https://thestockpicker2010.blogspot.com

https://stockmarketinvestorblog.blogspot.com

https://thestockpickingblog.blogspot.com

https://thevalueinvestorblog.blogspot.com

https://personalfinancetimes.blogspot.com

https://theeconomicanalyst.blogspot.com

https://mymoneymakingtipsblog.blogspot.com

https://weightlossdecrease.blogspot.com

AUTHOR'S FACEBOOK PAGE

https://facebook.com/stock.trader.39

TWITTER

@Jrlvt

LINKS TO SUPPORT THE AUTHOR'S WORK

SHOP AT THE AMAZON LINK BELOW TO SUPPORT AUTHOR'S WORK:

https://amzn.to/2gRrd9W

MAKE A PAYPAL CONTRIBUTION TO SUPPORT AUTHOR'S WORK:

https://paypal.me/JamesLynd

PERFECT THREADS CLOTHING COMPANY

Check out the author's clothing company at the link below, you can create your very own clothing / shirts; once inside the link, just click on the "CREATE' link to get started:

https://shop.spreadshirt.com/PerfectThreads

OTHER INFORMATION

The author has a Master of Business Administration degree with a concentration in Finance from the University of Baltimore and a Bachelor of Science Degree from Virginia Tech. In addition to having interests in money, investing and wealth, the author has interests in building businesses, e-commerce, sports, travel and organic gardening.

NOTES SECTION

NOTES SECTION

END

www.ingramcontent.com/pod-product-compliance
Lightning Source LLC
Chambersburg PA
CBHW050025230526
45470CB00003B/1133